REMINDING YOU OF HOW **LOVED** YOU ARE BY WAY OF LEGENDARY **K-DRAMA** QUOTES

나도 사랑해

A NOTE TO PASS ON

WRITTEN BY SHAI

나도 사랑해

A NOTE TO PASS ON

A NOTE TO PASS ON
"나도 사랑해"

Published by Stepping Stones Publishing
Copyright © Shai

The author asserts the moral right under the Copyright, Designs and Patents Act 1988 to be identified as the author of this work.

All Rights reserved. No part of this publication may be reproduced, stored in a retrieval system or transmitted, in any form or by any means without the prior consent
of the author, nor be otherwise circulated in any form of binding or cover other than that which it is published and without a similar condition being imposed on
the subsequent purchaser.

Copyright © 2023 Shai
All rights reserved.

ISBN: Paperback: 978-1-915862-08-2 | Hardback 978-1-915862-09-9

나도사랑해

A NOTE TO PASS ON

WRITTEN BY SHAI

If you're reading this book it means...

that you deserve to be reminded of
how loved you are every single day...

From

How to use this book

Everyday open this book to a random page, read the reminder that you land on.

This book is here to remind you how loved you are every single day - by way of quotes from some legendary Korean Dramas.

— Shai

나도 사랑해

A NOTE TO PASS ON

나도 사랑해

나도 사랑해

"I will protect you until the day I die, even if it means risking my own life." - from "Crash Landing on You"

나도 사랑해

"I don't want to be a momentary happiness in your life. I want to be your forever." - from "Healer"

나도 사랑해

"As long as you love someone, you have to try hard. Trying hard for someone makes life something worth trying at." - from "Because This Is My First Life"

나도 사랑해

"I think it was fate." - from
"The King Eternal Monarch

나도 사랑해

"I think I've fallen for you. That's why my heart hurts so much."- from "It's Okay to Not Be Okay"

"I will wait for you, no matter how long it takes." - from "Moon Lovers: Scarlet Heart Ryeo"

나도 사랑해

"I love you, not because of
who you are, but because of
who I am when I am with you."
- from "The Heirs"

나도 사랑해

"I will love you for a thousand years, and then for an eternity after that." - from "My Love From The Star"

나도 사랑해

"I will love you even in my
next life." - from "Goblin"

나도 사랑해

"I will stay by your side, always."
- from "Strong Woman Do Bong Soon"

나도 사랑해

"I will love you until the end of time." - from "The Legend of the Blue Sea"

"I will love you even if the world comes to an end." - from "Weightlifting Fairy Kim Bok-joo"

나도 사랑해

"I will love you even if the world turns against you." - from "Goblin"

"I will love you even if you can't love yourself." - from "Itaewon Class"

나도 사랑해

"I will love you even if I don't understand everything about you." - from "Hotel Del Luna"

나도 사랑해

"You are the only person who
can make me feel alive."
- from "W"

나도 사랑해

"I will love you until the stars stop shining and the seas dry up." - from "Crash Landing on You"

"I will love you even if you don't love me back." - from "Something in the Rain"

나도 사랑해

"I will love you even if you can't remember me." - from "Memory Lost"

"I will love you even if you don't believe in love." - from "Love Alarm"

나도 사랑해

"I will love you even in the darkest of times, because you are my light." - from "When the Camellia Blooms"

"I like you. I can't believe I am expressing this while mixing my noodles. I just want you to know how I feel. I don't want to cause any burden to you, so I'm not expecting your response."
– from "Start Up"

나도 사랑해

"I will love you even if you're not perfect, because you're perfect to me." - from "It's Okay to Not Be Okay"

"I will love you even if we can't be together, because you will always be in my heart."

- from "The King: Eternal Monarch"

나도 사랑해

"I will love you even if we have to say goodbye, because our love will live on forever."

 - from "Moonlight Drawn by Clouds"

"I will love you until the end of time, because you are my forever."

- from "The Legend of the Blue Sea"

나도 사랑해

"I will love you even if we face the toughest of challenges, because I know that together, we can overcome anything."

- from "Strong Woman Do Bong Soon"

나도 사랑해

"I will love you even if we come from different worlds, because our love knows no boundaries."

- from "My Love from the Star"

나도 사랑해

"I will love you even if we have to fight for our love, because it's worth fighting for." - from "Playful Kiss"

"I will love you even if we have to be apart, because distance can never change how much you mean to me." - from "While You Were Sleeping"

나도 사랑해

"I will love you even if we have to start over, because our love is worth a second chance."

- from "It's Okay to Not Be Okay"

"I will love you even if we have to face the toughest of challenges, because you make me stronger every day." - from "Heirs"

나도 사랑해

"I will love you even if we can't be together now, because I will wait for you, no matter how long it takes."

- from "Moon Lovers: Scarlet Heart Ryeo"

"I will love you even if you don't remember me, because the memories of our love will always stay in my heart."

- from "Memory Lost"

나도 사랑해

"I will love you even if you don't believe in love, because I will show you how much you are loved." - from
"Love Alarm"

"I will love you even if the world turns against you, because you are my world and I will always stand by you." - from "Goblin"

나도 사랑해

"I may not be the best, but I promise to love you with all my heart." - from "My Love from the Star"

나도 사랑해

"I will love you every single day, for the rest of my life."
- from "Crash Landing on You"

나도 사랑해

"You are my everything, my reason for living." - from "Healer"

나도 사랑해

"I will love you even if we have to be apart, because my love for you will never fade."

- from "Moon Lovers: Scarlet Heart Ryeo"

나도 사랑해

"I will love you even if you
can't love yourself, because I
will love you for the both of us."

- from "It's Okay to Not Be Okay"

나도 사랑해

"I will love you even if the world turns against you, because you are my world and I will always stand by you." - from "Goblin"

나도 사랑해

"You are my everything, my past, present and future."
- from "The Heirs"

나도 사랑해

"I will love you until the stars stop shining and the seas dry up."
- from "Crash Landing on You"

나도 사랑해

"I will wait for you, no matter how long it takes." - from "Moon Lovers: Scarlet Heart Ryeo"

"I will love you even if you don't remember me, because the memories of our love will always stay in my heart."

- from "Memory Lost"

나도 사랑해

"I will love you even if you don't believe in love, because I will show you how much you are loved."

- from "Love Alarm"

"I will love you even in the darkest of times, because you are my light."

- from "When the Camellia Blooms"

나도 사랑해

"I will love you until the end of time, because you are my forever."

- from "The Legend of the Blue Sea"

나도 사랑해

"I will love you even if we have to start over, because our love is worth a second chance." - from "It's Okay to Not Be Okay"

나도 사랑해

"I will love you even if we have to fight for our love, because it's worth fighting for." - from "Playful Kiss"

*"After meeting you, I always smiled.
You always made me smile."* - *from "The Red Sleeve"*

나도 사랑해

"You said our first encounter was on the worst terms. Not for me though. I saw a woman on the beach that day. She sat there for a long time, but all I could see was sadness in her eyes. And I couldn't get it out of my mind, so my eyes kept being drawn to her. But I never thought that I'd fall in love with her."

– from "Hometown Cha-Cha-Cha"

"You do not have to explain it. I know how you feel. I felt the same way. I missed you."
– from "Mr. Queen"

나도 사랑해

"If we are not from the same world, I will find you." – from "Moon Lovers: Scarlet Heart Ryeo"

"We can sit together like this and admire the flowers blooming and withering away every year. At night we can stargaze. On rainy days, we can listen to the rain falling in our yard together."
– from "The King's Affection"

나도 사랑해

"I wonder what it'd feel like to fall in love at first sight. But the moment I saw him, I felt it right away. Our hands brushed just briefly, but my heart began to pound.
Is this first love?"

– from "Snowdrop"

나도 사랑해

"You keep appearing in front of me and I keep getting tangled up with you. But you doing that is because of me, I think. I think I did something to give you hope. Okay. Let's date. I like you too."

– from "Reply 1988"

나도 사랑해

"You say that my love is a fantasy. You're wrong. It is real." – My Girlfriend Is A Gumiho

"Your two eyes were deep and as clear as the clearest of seas. I wanted to protect you. Wherever you wish to go, I will be by your side."

– from "The King's Affection"

나도 사랑해

"You probably have no idea what you mean to me in my life. You are my first love, my last love, and my life."

– from "18 Again"

"From spring to summer, from summer to fall, and from fall to winter, do you know when season changes? Do you know when winter ends and spring begins? I don't know when exactly my feeling for you started to grow."

– from "Romance Is A Bonus Book"

나도 사랑해

"I thought about it and realized life is short. I feel that my love will be longer than my life. That's why in this life, my love won't end." – from "The Legend Of The Blue Sea"

"How can I give up on you? I've finally found the one." – from "Something In The Rain"

나도 사랑해

*"I have a wish. I want you to love me.
Can I wish for that, too?" – from
 "Doom At Your Service"*

"How can I give up on you? I've finally found the one." – from *"Something In The Rain"*

나도 사랑해

"Love doesn't mean giving something up for the other person. But it means to achieve something" - from *"It's ok that's love"*

"Growing old together, what does it feel like? Together... I want to grow old with her" - from "My Love From Another Star"

나도 사랑해

"Love is all about patience."
- from "It's ok to not be ok"

You can cherish and care about people in different ways. Think about the different kinds of yellow. Even the same color can take different names depending on its chroma. The same goes for human emotions, such as affection...

- from "It's ok to not be ok"

나도 사랑해

"Saranghae... saranghandago!

Saranghandinikka!

Jjinjja, neomu, neomu saranghae...

Neaga saranghandane...

Ya! - from "It's ok to not be ok"

"I will love you until the stars stop shining and the seas dry up." - from "Crash Landing on You"

나도 사랑해

"I will wait for you, no matter how long it takes." - from "Moon Lovers: Scarlet Heart Ryeo"

"I will love you even if you don't remember me, because the memories of our love will always stay in my heart."

- from "Memory Lost"

나도 사랑해

"I will love you even if you don't believe in love, because I will show you how much you are loved."

- from "Love Alarm"

"I will love you even in the darkest of times, because you are my light."
- from "When the Camellia Blooms"

나도 사랑해

"I will love you until the end of time, because you are my forever." - from "The Legend of the Blue Sea"

"I will love you even if we have to start over, because our love is worth a second chance." - from "It's Okay to Not Be Okay"

나도 사랑해

"As long as you love someone, you have to try hard. Trying hard for someone makes life something worth trying at."
- from "Because This Is My First Life"

나도 사랑해

"I think it was fate." - from
"The King Eternal Monarch

나도 사랑해

"I will love you even if we have to fight for our love, because it's worth fighting for." - from "Playful Kiss"

나도 사랑해

"After meeting you, I always smiled. You always made me smile." - from "The Red Sleeve"

나도 사랑해

"You said our first encounter was on the worst terms. Not for me though. I saw a woman on the beach that day. She sat there for a long time, but all I could see was sadness in her eyes.

And I couldn't get it out of my mind, so my eyes kept being drawn to her. But I never thought that I'd fall in love with her." – from "Hometown Cha-Cha-Cha"

"You do not have to explain it. I know how you feel. I felt the same way. I missed you."
– from "Mr. Queen"

나도 사랑해

"If we are not from
the same world,
I will find you."

– from "Moon Lovers:
Scarlet Heart Ryeo"

"We can sit together like this and admire the flowers blooming and withering away every year. At night we can stargaze. On rainy days, we can listen to the rain falling in our yard together."
– from "The King's Affection"

나도 사랑해

"I will love you even if we face the toughest of challenges, because I know that together, we can overcome anything."

- from "Strong Woman Do Bong Soon"

"I will love you even if we come from different worlds, because our love knows no boundaries."

- from "My Love from the Star"

나도 사랑해

"I will love you even if we have to fight for our love, because it's worth fighting for." - from "Playful Kiss"

"I will love you even if we have to be apart, because distance can never change how much you mean to me." - from "While You Were Sleeping"

나도 사랑해

"I will love you even if we have to start over, because our love is worth a second chance."

- from "It's Okay to Not Be Okay"

"I will love you even if we have to face the toughest of challenges, because you make me stronger every day." - from "Heirs"

나도 사랑해

"I will love you even if we can't be together now, because I will wait for you, no matter how long it takes." - from "Moon Lovers: Scarlet Heart Ryeo"

"I will love you even if you don't remember me, because the memories of our love will always stay in my heart." - from "Memory Lost"

나도 사랑해

"I will love you even if you don't believe in love, because I will show you how much you are loved." - from "Love Alarm"

"I will love you even if the world turns against you, because you are my world and I will always stand by you." - from "Goblin"

나도 사랑해

"I may not be the best, but I promise to love you with all my heart."

- from "My Love from the Star"

"I will love you every single
day, for the rest of my life."
- from "Crash Landing
on You"

나도 사랑해

"You are my everything, my reason for living." - from "Healer"

"I will love you even if we have to be apart, because my love for you will never fade." - from "Moon Lovers: Scarlet Heart Ryeo"

나도 사랑해

"I will protect you until the day I die, even if it means risking my own life." - from "Crash Landing on You"

나도 사랑해

"I don't want to be a momentary happiness in your life. I want to be your forever." - from "Healer"

나도 사랑해

"I think I've fallen for you. That's why my heart hurts so much."
- from "It's Okay to Not Be Okay"

나도 사랑해

"I will wait for you, no matter how long it takes." - from "Moon Lovers: Scarlet Heart Ryeo"

나도 사랑해

"I love you, not because of who you are, but because of who I am when I am with you."
- from "The Heirs"

나도 사랑해

"I will love you for a thousand years, and then for an eternity after that." - from "My Love From the Star"

나도 사랑해

"I will love you even in my next life." - from "Goblin"

"I will stay by your side, always."
- from "Strong Woman Do Bong Soon"

나도 사랑해

"I will love you until the end of time." - from "The Legend of the Blue Sea"

"I will love you even if the world comes to an end." - from "Weightlifting Fairy Kim Bok-joo"

나도 사랑해

"I will love you even if the world turns against you." - from "Goblin"

"I will love you even if you can't love yourself." - from "Itaewon Class"

나도 사랑해

"I will love you even if I don't understand everything about you." - from "Hotel Del Luna"

"You are the only person who can make me feel alive." - from "W"

나도 사랑해

"I will love you until the stars stop shining and the seas dry up."
- from "Crash Landing on You"

"I will love you even if you don't love me back." - from "Something in the Rain"

나도 사랑해

"As long as you love someone, you have to try hard. Trying hard for someone makes life something worth trying at." - from "Because This Is My First Life"

"I think it was fate." - from "The King Eternal Monarch"

나도 사랑해

A NOTE TO PASS ON

나도사랑해

A NOTE TO PASS ON

WRITTEN BY SHAI

www.ingramcontent.com/pod-product-compliance
Lightning Source LLC
Chambersburg PA
CBHW041801160426
43191CB00001B/3